Your love is a river that flows through me
A fire that burns within my soul
It's a feeling that I cannot hide or flee
A love that makes me feel whole

Your touch ignites a passion deep
Within my heart, it beats for you
Your voice soothes me when I weep
I love everything that you do

In your eyes, I see a world of wonder
A world I want to explore and share
Together, we'll conquer every thunder
Our love, a bond that nothing can tear

Your beauty is like a rose in bloom
Your smile, the sun in the sky
My heart is yours, my love, assume
For you, I'll reach for the sky

Your laughter is music to my ears
Your touch, like a gentle breeze
My love for you, it never disappears
It only grows stronger with ease

You are the light in my darkest hour
The reason for my every breath
My love for you, it has the power
To conquer life and death

Love is a gift that I cherish
A precious treasure from above
It's a feeling that cannot perish
A bond that forever I'll love

With you, my heart beats faster
My soul sings with every touch
Together, we'll conquer disaster
Our love, it will never rust

You are the one that I adore
The reason for my every smile
My love for you, it's forevermore
It'll never fade or go out of style

So let us walk hand in hand
Through the storms and sunny weather
For with you, my love, I stand
Together, forever and ever

With every beat of my heart,
I feel the love we share.
It's a bond that cannot be torn apart,
A connection that's beyond compare.

You are my everything, my all,
My heart, my soul, my mate.
Together we stand tall,
Our love will never abate.

In your arms I feel safe and secure,
In your eyes I see forevermore.
You are the light that guides me home,
The one I'll love until I'm gone.

You came into my life,
And brought me light and joy.
My heart was once full of strife,
But now it's full of love, oh boy.

Your smile, your laugh, your touch,
They all make my heart sing.
I never thought I'd find this much,
Love that makes my heart ring.

You complete me in every way,
With you by my side, I can conquer the day.
I'm grateful for your love and grace,
Forever yours, in every place.

Our love is like a garden,
Growing stronger every day.
With every word and every pardon,
Our love grows in every way.

The seeds of our love were sown,
And now we watch it bloom.
Our love will never be alone,
It will never face any doom.

Together we tend to our love,
Watering it with care.
We know that it will rise above,
And flourish beyond compare.

Our love is like a garden,
Growing stronger every day.
With every kiss and every pardon,
Our love grows in every way.

You are the light of my life,
The one who makes everything right.
With you by my side,
I can conquer any strife.

Your love is like a warm embrace,
That keeps my heart beating with grace.
I cherish every moment with you,
For in your arms, I feel brand new.

In your eyes, I see the stars,
That twinkle and shine from afar.
Your smile is like a ray of light,
That brightens up my darkest night.

With you, I feel complete,
My heart's desire, my soulmate, my sweet.
Together, we will navigate life's journey,
With love as our guide, we'll never worry.

As the sun rises in the east,
My love for you will never cease.
Through the highs and the lows,
My love for you forever grows.

Your touch, your voice, your smile,
Makes my heart race for miles.
I am grateful to have you by my side,
My love for you, I cannot hide.

Your love is like a garden,
Filled with beauty and grace.
Each day, I am amazed,
By the depth of your embrace.

Your kindness, your passion, your soul,
Makes me feel whole.
I am grateful for every moment with you,
For in your love, I feel brand new.

I promise to love you forever,
Through the storms and the weather.
Together we will face life's challenges,
With love as our anchor, our balance.

You are my heart, my soul, my light,
My forever love, my delight.
With you, I feel complete,
Together we will never miss a beat.

My heart is yours, my love,
A gift I give to thee,
A precious thing that beats for you,
For all eternity.

With every breath I take,
My love for you grows more,
And every moment spent apart,
Is one I do deplore.

So take my heart, my darling,
And hold it close to you,
For in your gentle loving hands,
It will forever be true.

Your beauty takes my breath away,
Your grace, your charm, your poise,
With every passing day my love,
My passion only grows.

Your eyes, they shine like diamonds bright,
Your smile, it lights up my world,
With every touch, with every kiss,
My heart, it is unfurled.

And so I pledge my love to you,
My darling, sweet and true,
For in your arms, I find my peace,
My joy, my love, my due.

I love you more than words can say,
More than the stars above,
My heart is yours, forever true,
My one and only love.

With every breath, with every beat,
My love for you does grow,
And in your arms, I find my home,
Where all my troubles go.

Together we will face the world,
With courage and with grace,
And through the highs and through the lows,
Our love, it will embrace.

So take my hand, my love, my life,
And let us walk this way,
Together, hand in hand, in love,
Forever and a day.

You are the one who holds my heart,
The one I cannot bear to be apart.
Your gentle touch, your loving gaze,
Fills my heart with joy and amaze.

You are the one who brings me peace,
With you by my side, my fears release.
The sound of your voice, the warmth of your embrace,
Fills my soul with love and grace.

You are the one who makes me whole,
With you, I feel truly whole.
My love for you will never fade,
For you, I will always be your maid.

Our love story began with a glance,
A chance encounter that left me in a trance.
Your eyes met mine, and my heart skipped a beat,
I knew then that you were the one I'd always seek.

We shared laughs and tears, and life's ups and downs,
And through it all, our love never drowned.
Our love has grown stronger with each passing day,
And in your arms, I find my solace and my stay.

Our love story is one of passion and trust,
Of patience and understanding, and a love that must
Stand the test of time, and weather every storm,
For we are meant to be together, in love's warm.

A love so true, it knows no bounds,
With every kiss, our hearts resound.
Our love is like a rose in bloom,
It's beauty and fragrance, forever in tune.

A love so true, it fills our souls,
With every touch, our passion unfolds.
Our love is like a song in the air,
It's melody and rhythm, a love so rare.

A love so true, it stands the test of time,
With every moment, our love's sublime.
Our love is like a flame in the dark,
It's warmth and light, forever in our heart.

Your smile is like the sun that shines so bright,
It fills my heart with warmth and light.
I could gaze upon your face for hours,
Lost in the magic of your powers.

Your smile is like a beacon in the night,
Guiding me towards all that's right.
With you by my side, I'm never alone,
For your love is the truest I've ever known.

My heart beats faster when you're near,
I feel alive when you're here.
Your touch ignites a flame in me,
A love so strong, it's meant to be.

My heart belongs to you alone,
With you, my love, my heart is home.
Forever and always, we'll be together,
Our love will never fade or wither.

I love you more than words can say,
My love for you grows stronger each day.
You're the sunshine on a cloudy day,
The one who makes everything okay.

In your arms, I find my peace,
With you, my heart will never cease.
You're my one and only, my heart and soul,
Without you, my love, I'd be incomplete and
whole.

You're the one I love, my heart's desire,
The one who sets my soul on fire.
I can't imagine life without you,
With every breath, my love for you grows true.

Together we'll face life's ups and downs,
With you, my love, I'm never alone.
I'll hold your hand through thick and thin,
Forever and always, our love will win.

You are the sun that brightens my day,
The moon that guides me on my way.
You are the stars that light up my night,
The breeze that cools me with delight.

You are the laughter that fills my heart,
The tears that we shed when we're apart.
You are the one I want by my side,
The love that I'll always abide.

My love for you is like the ocean,
Vast and deep, and always in motion.
It ebbs and flows, but never dies,
And in your arms, I feel alive.

My love for you is like the sky,
Expansive, infinite, and so high.
It spreads its wings and takes flight,
And in your eyes, I find delight.

My love for you is like the earth,
Steadfast, strong, and full of worth.
It grounds me, and gives me strength,
And in your love, I find my length.

You are my forever, my one and only,
The love that I've been waiting for, so holy.
You light up my world, with your smile,
And in your arms, I feel worthwhile.

You are the love that fills my heart,
The reason why I can't stay apart.
You are the soulmate that I seek,
The one that makes my life complete.

So here I am, with this love poem,
Telling you how much you mean to me, and how much you have
grown.
Together, we'll walk the path of life,
Hand in hand, forever husband and wife.

Our love is like the stars above,
Forever shining bright,
A never-ending story,
Of two souls entwined in light.

Through good times and bad,
Our love remains steadfast,
A bond unbreakable,
That will always last.

With every beat of our hearts,
Our love grows stronger still,
A flame that burns eternal,
A love that always will.

The beauty of your love,
Is like a rose in bloom,
So delicate and precious,
A gift from heaven's room.

With every breath I take,
My heart beats just for you,
For you are the one I love,
My heart, my soul, my true.

In your eyes, I see a light,
A flame that never fades,
A love that shines forever,
A love that never fades.

So let us cherish this love,
And hold it close each day,
For the beauty of your love,
Will never fade away.

My heart's desire is simple,
To love you more each day,
To hold you in my arms,
And never let you stray.

With every moment that passes,
My love for you grows strong,
A bond that will never break,
A love that will never wrong.

I promise to cherish you always,
To be there through thick and thin,
To be your rock and shelter,
And love you until the end.

So let us embrace this love,
And cherish it forevermore,
For my heart's desire is simple,
To love you forevermore.

My love for you is like the sun,
Always shining bright and true,
No matter where you go or what you do,
My love will always be with you.

My heart beats for you, my sweet,
In every moment, every beat,
With each breath I take, I know,
My love for you will only grow.

No storm or tempest can shake our love,
It's steadfast and unwavering like a dove,
Through thick and thin, we'll always be,
Together, forever, just you and me.

My love for you is boundless,
Like the ocean deep and wide,
It flows and ebbs and never stops,
A force that cannot be denied.

Your beauty takes my breath away,
Your laughter lights up my day,
I'm lost in the depths of your eyes,
With you, my heart forever lies.

I vow to love you till the end of time,
To cherish you forever and be mine,
Our love will conquer every fear,
Together, we have nothing to fear.

Your love is like an eternal flame,
Burning bright and never tamed,
It lights up my life and fills my soul,
Making me feel whole and in control.

In your arms, I find my peace,
In your embrace, my worries cease,
You are the light that guides my way,
Through the night and into the day.

With every kiss and every touch,
I feel your love, I feel so much,
Our love is like a never-ending story,
Filled with passion, joy, and glory.

Like a flame that never fades
Our love burns bright and strong
Through the trials and the shade
We keep moving on

You are the light that guides me
Through the darkness of the night
Together we are free
To soar on wings of flight

Forever in your embrace
I find my heart's true home
My love for you will never erase
Through the years as they roam

Our passion ignites and inspires
A fire that will never die
Our love is the ultimate desire
A flame that will always fly

You are the song in my heart
A melody that never ends
With you, my love, I can start
A journey that never bends

Every moment spent with you
Is a symphony of bliss
Our love so pure and true
Like a sweet serenade, we kiss

Together we dance in harmony
Two souls that intertwine
Your love has set me free
My heart forever thine

In your arms, I find solace
A refuge from the world outside
Our love is an eternal promise
A bond that will never subside

From the moment our eyes met
My heart knew you were the one
With you, I'll never forget
The love that we have begun

We are soulmates, you and I
Two halves of a whole
Our love will never die
As we journey through life's tolls

In your arms, I find safety
A place to call my own
Our love is the sweetest melody
A symphony of love we've sown

With you, I'm complete
A puzzle piece that fits just right
Our love is an endless feat
A journey that takes flight

My love for you is like a river that flows,
Constant and true, wherever it goes.
Like the sun that rises and sets each day,
My love for you will never fade away.

In your arms, I find my safe haven,
Where I can rest and feel forgiven.
Your love is like a melody in my heart,
That plays a tune that never departs.

My heart beats for you, my love,
It sings a song of passion and desire.
You are the one I've been dreaming of,
My soulmate, my heart's true fire.

In your eyes, I see a future so bright,
Filled with love, laughter, and delight.
In your embrace, I find my home,
Where I can be myself, and never alone.

You are my forever Valentine,
The one who makes my heart shine.
You light up my life like the sun,
And with you, my love, I feel so fun.

In your arms, I find my peace,
Where all my worries and fears cease.
Your love is like a sweet melody,
That fills my heart with endless glee.

From the moment I saw you,
I knew my heart was yours to woo.
Your beauty, your grace, your charm,
To me, you were a rare and precious charm.

As I gazed into your eyes so blue,
My heart skipped a beat or two.
In that moment, I knew it was true,
That my heart belonged to only you.

Our love is like a flame,
Burning bright, with no shame.
Through life's ups and downs,
Our love will never let us drown.

In your arms, I find my strength,
Where I can overcome any length.
Our love is like a storybook tale,
One that will never grow stale.

It was such a day;
My time is up.
It suddenly appeared before my eyes
Your beautiful face.
And my heart burned
My palms were sweaty.
An intense hive hum
I covered my ears.
I reached for my cigarette softly;
Add to my lazy life.
I died that day, my rose.
I will not die again."

"Whenever I think of you
A gazelle descends to drink water
I see the meadows growing.

every evening with you
Green olive
a piece of blue sea
takes me.

as we think of you
I plant roses where my hand touches
I give water to the horses
I love mountains more."

You are my sunshine in the rain,
My hope in times of pain.
Your love is the sweetest thing,
A melody that makes my heart sing.

Your smile lights up my darkest days,
And your touch sends me in a daze.
I love you more than words can say,
And I'll cherish you every day.

With every beat of my heart,
I feel your love, and it's a work of art.
You make my life complete,
And without you, my heart skips a beat.

Your love is like a precious gem,
Something I want to hold onto and never condemn.
I'll love you until the end of time,
And every day I'll make you mine.

Your eyes are like a window to your soul,
And your heart is where I want to call home.
I'll love you until the end of time,
And every day, I'll make you mine.

Your touch ignites a fire within,
A love that's pure and free from sin.
I'll cherish you with all my heart,
And we'll never be apart.

When I see you, my heart takes flight,
My soul alights with pure delight.
The world fades away, and all I see
Is the light in your eyes, shining on me.

I never knew love could be this sweet,
A feeling so strong, it knocks me off my feet.
But here I am, head over heels,
Falling deeper in love with every feel.

You are the light that guides me home,
The fire that warms me to the bone.
Your love is a balm that soothes my soul,
A love that makes me feel whole.

I never thought I'd find someone like you,
A love so pure, so strong, so true.
But here you are, my heart's desire,
The love I'll cherish, and never tire.

My love for you is like the sea,
Vast and endless, wild and free.
It ebbs and flows, but never fades,
A love that never will be swayed.

With every breath, I feel your touch,
A love that's pure, and oh so much.
I'll cherish you forevermore,
My love, my life, my everything, and more.

My love, my everything,
You are the sun in my sky,
The beat in my heart,
The twinkle in my eye.

With you by my side,
I can conquer any fear,
For your love is my strength,
And your touch, so dear.

I cherish every moment,
Every memory we share,
For in your arms,
I find solace and care.

My love, my everything,
I promise to cherish you,
For all the days of my life,
And beyond, forever true.

Forever in love,
Our hearts entwine,
As we walk hand in hand,
Through the sands of time.

You are my soulmate,
My rock, my guide,
With you by my side,
I can face the world with pride.

I thank the stars above,
For bringing us together,
For in your embrace,
I find love, joy and pleasure.

Forever in love,
We will stand strong,
For in each other's hearts,
We forever belong.

A love so pure,
It shines like the sun,
A bond so strong,
It can never be undone.

In your eyes I see,
The depth of your soul,
In your arms I feel,
The warmth of your hold.

With every kiss we share,
Our love grows stronger,
With every word we speak,
Our bond lasts longer.

A love so pure,
It surpasses all,
A flame that burns bright,
Even in the darkest of halls.

My heart sings a song for you,
A melody so sweet and true.
It beats to the rhythm of your name,
And I know my love will never wane.

With every breath, I long for you,
My love for you forever true.
You are the sunshine in my day,
And in your arms is where I'll stay.

I will love you until the end of time,
Our love is eternal, forever sublime.
You are the one who makes my heart sing,
And every moment with you is a precious thing.

Your touch sends shivers down my spine,
And I know that you are mine, all mine.
Together we will conquer the world,
And our love will never grow old.

You are the love of my life,
My soulmate, my forever wife.
I promise to love you forever and always,
Through the good times and the tough days.

You are the light in my darkness,
The one who fills my heart with happiness.
I will cherish you until the end of time,
And together we will make our love shine.

You are the fire that burns in my soul,
The one who makes my heart whole.
I long to be with you every day,
And I know our love will never fade away.

Your smile is like sunshine on a rainy day,
And your touch sends my troubles away.
I am blessed to have you by my side,
And I will love you until the end of time.

You are my forever love,
Sent to me from the heavens above.
I will cherish you until the end of time,
And our love will continue to shine.

You are the one who completes me,
The one who sets my spirit free.
Together we will conquer the world,
And our love will never grow old.

Your eyes, they are the stars
That light up my darkest nights
And your smile, it's the sun
That warms my soul and ignites

A flame inside my heart
That burns for you alone
For you are my everything
And my love for you has grown

With each passing day
My affection only deepens
And I thank the stars above
For bringing us together as kin

So here's to us, my love
To the memories we'll make
And to the unbreakable bond
That nothing can ever shake

In your arms I find peace
And in your embrace I'm whole
For you are the missing piece
That completes my heart and soul

Your laughter is my melody
Your touch my sweetest song
And in your eyes I see
The love that keeps me strong

I vow to cherish you always
And to hold you tight each day
For you are my forever love
And my heart will never stray

So let's dance together, my love
In this beautiful journey called life
For with you by my side
I know we'll conquer any strife

Your love is like a rose
That blooms with every passing day
And just like the flower grows
My love for you will never fade away

Your touch is like a breeze
That brings peace to my soul
And in your arms I find ease
For your love makes me whole

I thank the stars above
For bringing you into my life
And for filling it with love
And endless moments of delight

So here's to us, my love
To the memories we'll make
For with you by my side
I know my heart will never break.

In love's embrace I find my peace,
Where worries cease and joys increase.
With every beat my heart does race,
For in your arms I've found my place.

Your eyes that sparkle like the sun,
A smile that brightens everyone,
The love you give, a precious gift,
My heart and soul you've helped to lift.

So here I stand, before your grace,
In love's embrace I've found my place.
Together we'll weather every storm,
Our love forever, forever warm.

In this world of endless dreams,
You're the one that my heart deems,
As my soulmate, my one true love,
Sent to me from high above.

Your gentle touch, your tender kiss,
I long for every moment like this,
To be with you is all I seek,
My love for you, eternal and meek.

In your eyes, I see my future,
A life together, forever and ever,
Through thick and thin, we'll never part,
My soulmate, forever in my heart.

My love for you is like the sea,
Endless and vast, forever to be,
A force of nature, unrelenting and true,
My heart beats only for you.

The sun may rise, the sun may set,
But my love for you will never forget,
The moments we've shared, the memories we've made,
My love for you will never fade.

In your embrace, I find my home,
A place where my heart can roam,
With you, my love, I feel complete,
My soulmate, my heart's eternal beat.

So here's my promise, my love divine,
To cherish you until the end of time,
Together we'll stand, hand in hand,
Our love, forever and always grand.

My love for you is like the sky,
So vast, so endless, and so high.
My heart beats only for you,
My love, forever, pure and true.

With each breath, I feel your name,
With each step, I know our flame.
Forever, we shall be entwined,
Our love, a bond, so unconfined.

In every moment, I will cherish,
Our love, so bright, so divine.
For in your arms, my heart will flourish,
And our love will forever shine.

In every moment, I am struck,
By the beauty of you, my love, my luck.
Your eyes, like stars, so bright and clear,
Your smile, so warm, so dear.

With each touch, I feel your soul,
With each kiss, I am made whole.
My heart beats only for you,
My love, so pure, so true.

In every season, through every strife,
My love for you will light my life.
For in your embrace, I find my home,
And in your heart, I know I belong.

In the depths of my heart, I feel,
A love for you, so strong, so real.
Like the ocean, so vast and wide,
My love for you, will never subside.

In every moment, I am blessed,
For in your love, I find my rest.
With each touch, I am renewed,
My love for you, forever true.

Through every joy, through every pain,
My love for you, will always remain.
For in your eyes, I see my fate,
And in your heart, I find my mate.

So let us cherish, this love so deep,
And in each other's arms, let us sleep.
For in our love, we find our way,
And in each other, we find our stay.

Your love is a gentle breeze,
That lifts me up when I am down,
Your love is a warm embrace,
That fills my heart with a joyful sound.

Your love is a shining star,
That guides me through the darkest night,
Your love is a soothing balm,
That heals my wounds and makes things right.

Your love is the sweetest song,
That lingers in my heart all day long,
Your love is a precious gift,
That I cherish more than anything.

I choose you, my love,
In every moment, every day,
For you are the light in my life,
That brightens up my way.

I choose you, my love,
For the way you make me feel,
For the laughter and the joy,
That you bring into my world so real.

I choose you, my love,
For the passion and the fire,
For the way you stir my soul,
And ignite my heart's desire.

I choose you, my love,
For the love that we share,
For the way we complement each other,
And the way we make a perfect pair.

My heart sings a symphony,
Every time you come near,
Your smile, your touch, your voice,
Make my heart skip a beat, my dear.

My heart sings a symphony,
With every breath that I take,
For your love is the melody,
That keeps my heart awake.

My heart sings a symphony,
That echoes through the night,
For your love is the harmony,
That fills my world with light.

My heart sings a symphony,
That only you can hear,
For your love is the conductor,
That makes my heart sincere.

My heart beats for you, my love
It skips a beat when you're around
You fill my life with joy and bliss
My soul is yours, forever bound

Your smile lights up my darkest days
Your touch sends shivers down my spine
I'm grateful for the love we share
And glad that you are mine

I promise to love you, always and forever
Through every storm and every weather
My heart belongs to you, my dear
And with you, I have nothing to fear

You are my sunshine, my love
The light that guides me through the dark
You bring warmth to my coldest nights
And ignite a flame within my heart

Your beauty is beyond compare
Your grace and charm, a rare delight
I'm so thankful for the love we share
And for the joy you bring into my life

I promise to cherish you, forever and always
To love you more and more with each passing day
You are the one that makes my heart sing
And with you, I have everything.

A love that will last forevermore
That's what we have, my love, for sure
Our hearts beat as one, in perfect harmony
And I know that our love will stand the test of time, eternally

Your smile brightens up my world
Your touch ignites a flame in my heart
I'll cherish you, always and forever
Until death do us part

With you, I've found a love that's pure and true
A love that's strong, and steadfast, and new
I'll love you through the good times and the bad
And together, we'll conquer the world, hand in hand.

I love you more than words can say,
You make me feel alive every day.
My heart is yours forevermore,
Together we'll walk through life's door.

With every breath I take, I swear,
My love for you will always be there.
I'll cherish you until the end of time,
Together, our love will always shine.

My heart beats for you alone,
Your love has captured every tone.
My soul is yours, forevermore,
In your arms, I feel secure.

I love the way you make me feel,
With you, everything seems real.
Your touch, your kiss, your gentle embrace,
My heart's desire, my saving grace.

Your love is like music to my ears,
A symphony that soothes my fears.
With you, my heart sings a beautiful tune,
Love's sweet melody, that I never want to lose.

Every moment spent with you,
Is a precious gift, so pure and true.
Together, we'll dance to love's sweet beat,
Two hearts entwined, forever complete.

You are the sunshine in my life,
My reason to smile, my joy and delight.
Your love is like a warm embrace,
A light that shines on my face.

With you, I feel like I can fly,
Through life's journey, you're my guide.
I love you more with each passing day,
Forever and always, my love, I'll stay.

Our love is like a flower that blooms,
Through life's challenges, it still consumes.
It grows stronger with each passing day,
A love that lasts, come what may.

In your arms, I feel complete,
Together, our love will never deplete.
I'll love you until the end of time,
My heart is yours, forever thine.

In your eyes, I see the stars,
In your heart, I find my home,
You are the light that guides me,
And with you, I am never alone.

Your touch is like a gentle breeze,
That stirs my soul and sets me free,
With every kiss, I am complete,
For in your arms, I find my peace.

With every breath, my love for you,
Grows stronger, deeper, and true,
For you are the one I adore,
The one I long to hold forevermore.

In your smile, I find my joy,
In your laughter, I find my peace,
For you are the one I cherish,
The one who makes my heart sing.

I am lost in your embrace,
As I gaze into your eyes,
For in you, I find my soulmate,
The one who makes my heart rise.

You are the light that shines my path,
The one who fills my life with love,
For in your arms, I find my strength,
And in your heart, I find my home.

With every beat of my heart,
I think of you, my love,
For you are the one who brings me joy,
The one who fits me like a glove.

I am yours, and you are mine,
Forever, we will be entwined,
For in each other, we have found,
A love that is truly profound.

My heart belongs to you, my love,
A treasure that is yours alone,
Forever bound, like hand in glove,
A love that's truly set in stone.

Your eyes, so bright, like shining stars,
Illuminate my world with light,
My soul is yours, both near and far,
Forever bound in sweet delight.

Your touch ignites a fiery flame,
That burns within my very core,
With you beside me, I proclaim,
My love, you're all I'm living for.

Our love is like a rose in bloom,
A beauty that will never fade,
A love that's strong, like a monsoon,
And never ever will it shade.

The love we share is deep and true,
It spans the distance of all time,
A love that's rare, a love that's new,
And yet it feels so familiar, so sublime.

Our hearts beat as one, in perfect sync,
Our souls intertwined, forever bound,
A love that's endless, without a kink,
A love that's eternal, without a sound.

You are my sunshine on a cloudy day,
The light that guides me through the dark,
You are the reason for my smile,
The one who holds the key to my heart.

Your love is like a warm embrace,
A shelter from the stormy gale,
With you beside me, I can face,
Any challenge, any trial, any tale.

You are the missing piece to my puzzle,
The one who makes me whole and complete,
Your love is pure, and without any hustle,
Together we make a love that's so sweet.

A love so true, it knows no bounds,
It fills my heart and echoes through the sounds,
Of every whisper and every kiss,
I'm lost in you, I'm in pure bliss.

The way you look at me with your eyes,
Sends shivers down my spine and makes me sigh,
I'm drawn to you like a moth to a flame,
My heart beats faster at the sound of your name.

Your touch, your smile, your gentle embrace,
All these things I cannot replace,
I love you more than words can say,
And I'll love you more with each passing day.

Forever and always, my heart belongs to you,
Through the ups and downs, we'll see this love
through,
Through every trial, through every test,
I'll be here for you, I'll give you my best.

You are my light in the darkest of days,
You bring me joy in so many ways,
I am blessed to have you by my side,
My love for you will never subside.

Your beauty, your grace, your heart so kind,
All these things I hold dear in my mind,
I love you more than words can say,
And I'll love you more with each passing day.

The power of love is an amazing thing,
It can make your heart soar and make it sing,
It can heal the wounds of a broken heart,
And give a new beginning, a brand new start.

With you by my side, I feel so alive,
Your love gives me strength to survive,
Through every obstacle, through every trial,
I'll be here for you, I'll walk every mile.

Your laughter, your smile, your touch so sweet,
All these things make my heart skip a beat,
I love you more than words can say,
And I'll love you more with each passing day.

A promise of love, I make to you,
To love you always, to always be true,
To be there for you through thick and thin,
To never let you go, to hold you within.

With you in my life, I feel complete,
My heart is full, it's no longer a seat,
Of emptiness and loneliness and despair,
With you by my side, I have nothing to fear.

Your love, your kindness, your gentle soul,
All these things make my heart whole,
I love you more than words can say,
And I'll love you more with each passing day.

The beauty of love is a wondrous thing,
It can make your heart sing and make it ring,
With joy and happiness and pure delight,
It can fill your soul and make everything right.

With you in my life, I feel so blessed,
My heart is full, it's no longer a mess,
Of pain and sorrow and regret,
With you by my side, I have nothing to fret.

Your beauty, your charm, your grace so divine,
All these things make my heart shine,
I love you more than words can say,
And I'll love you more with each passing day.

In your arms, I feel so warm
Protected from life's raging storm
Your love is like a guiding light
Leading me through the darkest night

I can't imagine life without you
My heart beats only for you
You are the reason for my smile
I'll love you forever, mile by mile

My heart beats only for you
Your love is my heart's desire
My soul sings when I'm with you
My passion for you will never expire

Your smile lights up my day
Your touch ignites my soul
Your love takes my breath away
With you, I feel whole

Forever and always, my love
I'll stand by your side
With you, I'm complete
My heart is open wide

In your arms, I find peace
Your love is my sanctuary
With you, I'm truly blessed
Together, we are meant to be

Our love story is a tale to be told
It started with a spark, now it's gold
We've weathered the storms of life
Together, we've overcome all strife

With each passing day, I love you more
You're the one that I adore
Our love is a bond that can't be broken
Our future together is a promise spoken

Love is a beautiful thing
It makes my heart sing
Your love is a treasure
I'll cherish it forever

Your eyes, they captivate me
Your smile, it sets me free
Your love, it completes me
Together, we are meant to be

In your embrace, I feel complete,
My heart beats with a steady beat,
Your touch ignites a fiery heat,
A love that's strong and ever sweet.

In your eyes, I see my world,
A future bright, with joy unfurled,
Together, we're a perfect swirl,
A love that's true, a priceless pearl.

With every breath, I love you more,
Our bond unbreakable, at its core,
Forever and always, I adore,
My love for you, an endless store.

Your smile is like the morning sun,
It warms my heart, my day begun,
In your eyes, I see my fun,
A love that's pure, not just a pun.

Your laughter is a joyful sound,
My heart leaps up, with joy abound,
In your arms, I'm safe and sound,
A love that's strong, forever bound.

My love for you, an endless stream,
In your presence, I always gleam,
Together, we're a perfect team,
A love that's real, not just a dream.

In your kiss, I taste pure bliss,
My heart sings with a love that's amiss,
Without you, it's a loveless abyss,
With you, my life's a sweet reminisce.

Your touch ignites a passionate fire,
My soul ablaze with a burning desire,
Together, we can conquer any quagmire,
A love that's real, not just a satire.

My heart beats for you, day and night,
With you, I see a future bright,
A love that's true, a shining light,
My love for you, an endless sight.

The way you move, so effortless and free,
Like a bird soaring high above the trees.
Your grace and beauty take my breath away,
And I'm drawn to you in every single way.

Your smile, your laugh, your gentle touch,
All fill my heart with joy and such.
I cherish every moment spent with you,
And hope our love will always be true.

Your eyes, so deep and full of light,
They shine like stars on a clear night.
I could get lost in their endless gaze,
And spend forever in a love-filled daze.

Your eyes reveal the depths of your soul,
And every time I see them, my heart feels whole.
I'm grateful for the love that we share,
And the way you show me that you care.

My heart beats for you, my love,
A rhythm that's true and pure as a dove.
You are the light in my darkest night,
The hope that guides me towards the light.

Your touch is like a gentle breeze,
That sweeps me away with such ease.
I long to hold you close and never let go,
And cherish the love we've come to know.

The beauty of your love is like a rose,
So delicate and lovely, it grows and grows.
Your love is like a warm embrace,
A comforting hug in a hectic race.

Your love is like a gentle stream,
That flows and flows with a peaceful gleam.
I'm grateful for the love you give,
And for the way you help me to live.

Together forever, our love will last,
A bond that's strong and built to last.
I'll always be there by your side,
And cherish every moment, every ride.

Our love is like a flame that burns so bright,
And guides us through even the darkest night.
I'm grateful for the love we share,
And for the way you show me that you care.

My love for you is like a rose,
Fragrant, delicate, and sweet,
It blooms and blossoms every day,
And makes my heart skip a beat.

Your smile is like the sunshine,
That warms me to my core,
Your laughter is like music,
That I can't help but adore.

You are the missing piece of my puzzle,
The answer to my prayer,
I thank the stars every night,
That you are always there.

I see your face in every flower,
In every tree, and every star,
You are the light that guides me,
No matter where I am.

Your love is like a river,
That flows into my heart,
It nourishes me with tenderness,
And never lets me part.

You are my one and only,
The love of my life so true,
I thank the heavens every day,
For bringing me to you.

The sight of you takes my breath away,
Your beauty is beyond compare,
You light up my world like the sun,
And make me feel like I'm flying in the air.

Your touch is like magic,
It sends shivers down my spine,
Your love is the greatest gift,
That I could ever hope to find.

I'll cherish you forever,
And hold you in my heart,
I'll love you more each passing day,
Till death do us part.

My Love, My Life
My love, my life, my everything,
You are the song that my heart sings.
In your eyes I see the stars,
And your smile takes away my scars.
You are the sunshine in my day,
The moonlight that guides my way.
In your arms I find my peace,
And all my worries seem to cease.

My love for you will never fade,
For you, my heart was made.
With every breath that I take,
My love for you will never break.

You Are My Forever
You are my forever, my soulmate,
The one I want to be with till the end of fate.
Your love is like a beautiful melody,
That fills my heart with so much glee.
In your arms, I find my home,
A place where I am never alone.
Your love is like a warm embrace,
That takes away all my fears and grace.

My love for you will never die,
For you, I would climb the highest sky.
With every beat of my heart,
I promise to love you till we're apart.

Love Is All We Need
Love is all we need to survive,
To keep our hearts and souls alive.
It's the bond that keeps us together,
Through all the storms that we may weather.
Your love is like a breath of fresh air,
A feeling that's beyond compare.
In your eyes, I see my future,
A world where love is the only sutra.

My love for you is infinite,
A feeling that will never quit.
With every moment that we share,
I know that love will always be there.

A Love Like Ours
A love like ours is rare to find,
A bond that's strong, true and kind.
Your love is like a ray of light,
That fills my heart with so much delight.
In your embrace, I find my peace,
A love that never seems to cease.
Your touch ignites a fire in me,
A passion that's pure and free.

My love for you will never wane,
For you, my heart will always remain.
With every beat of my heart,
I promise to love you till we're apart.

Love Is Eternal
Love is eternal, a bond that never fades,
A feeling that's beyond all shades.
Your love is like a work of art,
A masterpiece that's close to my heart.
In your eyes, I see my dreams,
A world where love is all it seems.
Your touch is like a gentle breeze,
That takes away all my worries and ease.

My love for you is boundless,
A feeling that's so precious.
With every breath that I take,
I promise to love you till we're awake.

The one I love is like the sun
That shines so bright and true
With each and every passing day
My love for them just grew

Their smile is like the morning dew
That glistens on the grass
Their laugh is like a symphony
That fills my heart with mass

I am so blessed to have them here
To cherish and to hold
They are my heart, my soul, my life
My love will never fold

In your eyes, I see the stars
That light up my dark skies
In your embrace, I find my peace
And all my fears subside

Your touch ignites a fire within
That burns with passion true
I know that I am meant for you
And you are meant for me too

Together we'll walk hand in hand
Through life's unpredictable twists and turns
Our love will stand the test of time
And forever we'll be yours

My heart's desire, my sweetest dream
Is to be with you, my love supreme
Your gentle touch, your loving gaze
Sets my heart ablaze

I cherish every moment spent with you
And every memory we create anew
Our love is like a garden in bloom
With fragrant flowers and sweet perfume

My heart beats with the rhythm of your soul
As we dance together, two halves of a whole
My love for you is pure and true
Forever and always, I'll be here for you

In your eyes I see the stars
That light up the night sky
And in your smile I find
The sun that warms my heart

Your touch sets my heart ablaze
And your kiss ignites my soul
With you, I feel alive and free
And my love for you will never grow old

In every moment spent with you
My heart beats a little faster
For in your arms I find my peace
And in your love I find my rapture

With every breath I take,
My love for you grows stronger
And every day that passes by
I realize I couldn't love you any longer

Like a flower that blooms in spring
My love for you blossoms each day
And like the sun that shines so bright
You light up my life in every way

You are the beat that keeps my heart alive,
The melody that makes my soul thrive
In your arms, I find my true home,
My heart will always belong to you alone.

You are my sunshine on a cloudy day,
The warmth that makes my troubles fade
away.
In your embrace, I find my peace,
My love for you will never cease.

With every breath I take,
I feel your love so deep,
Like the ocean waves that crash ashore,
My love for you will never sleep.

In the depths of my heart,
A love so true does start.
With each passing day,
My love for you does not sway.

Your smile, your touch, your kiss,
All fill me with pure bliss.
I am grateful for your love,
A blessing from above.

Together we will stay,
Through every night and day.
With a love so true,
I promise to always be there for you.

In your arms, I find my home,
A place where I am never alone.
With you by my side,
I feel like I can conquer any tide.

Your love fills my soul,
Making me feel whole.
Together we are unstoppable,
A love so true and irreplaceable.

Through the ups and downs,
Our love will never drown.
Forever in love,
Together we will rise above.

You are the beat of my heart,
The rhythm that sets me apart.
In your embrace, I find solace,
A love so pure and flawless.

With each passing day,
My love for you does not sway.
You are the one I adore,
Forever and always, now and evermore.

I thank the stars above,
For sending you to me with love.
In your eyes, I see my future,
A love so true and pure.

Together we will walk,
Hand in hand, heart in heart.
You are my heart,
And I promise to never be apart.

The beauty of your love,
Is like a gift from above.
It fills me with joy and delight,
And makes everything feel so right.

Your love is like a flower,
That blooms with each passing hour.
It is a treasure that I hold dear,
A love that will always be near.

In your arms, I find peace,
And all my troubles cease.
I am grateful for your love,
A blessing sent from above.

With you by my side,
I am ready to face the world with pride.
For the beauty of your love,
Is a gift that I will forever cherish above.

In your eyes, I see the stars,
And in your heart, I find my home.
You are the light that guides me through,
The one I love, and call my own.

Your smile is like the sun,
It brightens up my day.
Your touch is like a gentle breeze,
It sweeps my cares away.

Your love is like a rose,
So beautiful and rare.
It fills my heart with joy and hope,
And takes away my care.

My love for you is like a flame,
That burns so bright and true.
It warms my heart and lights my way,
And leads me back to you.

I love the way you look at me,
With eyes so bright and blue.
It makes my heart skip a beat,
And fills my soul anew.

My love for you is like a river,
Flowing deep and wide.
It carries me along with it,
And fills me up inside.

You are the sun that warms my face,
The moon that lights my way.
You are the stars that guide me home,
And the love that makes me stay.

I love the way you laugh and play,
The way you smile and sing.
You make my heart feel light and gay,
And fill my life with spring.

My love for you is like a song,
So sweet and pure and true.
It lifts me up and carries me,
And leads me back to you.

I love you more than words can say,
More than stars in the sky.
You are the love that fills my heart,
And the reason that I try.

In your eyes, I see the stars
And in your touch, the moon
My heart sings with joy
Whenever I am with you

You are the sunshine in my life
The one who makes everything right
I promise to love and cherish you
From morning until night

Your love is the light in my life
That guides me through each day
And with you by my side
I know that anything is possible and okay

Forever and always, my love
I vow to cherish you
For in your embrace
I have found my heart's true bliss.

In your eyes, I see the stars
And in your smile, the sun
I am forever grateful
That our paths have become one

Your touch ignites a fire
That burns within my soul
I am forever yours
Until the end of time unfolds

I never knew what love was
Until I met you, my sweet dove
Now every moment without you
Feels like a life without love

Your beauty is like a rose
Fragrant and divine
And with you by my side
I feel like I can climb any climb

I promise to love you always
And cherish you forevermore
For in your arms, my dear love
I have found my heart's true home.

Your eyes are like the stars above,
Your lips so sweet, they taste of love,
I'm lost in you, my heart's aflame,
I'll love you forever, that's my aim.

With every kiss, with every touch,
I feel your love, I feel so much,
You're all I need, you're all I want,
I'll love you forever, I'll never stop.

In love's embrace, I find my peace,
My heart is full, my joy released,
Your arms around me, holding tight,
I'm safe with you, all through the night.

Your love's a fire, burning bright,
I'm drawn to you, with all my might,
In every moment, every way,
I'll love you more, with each new day.

Together we're unstoppable,
Our love is strong, unbreakable,
In love's embrace, we'll always be,
Forever bound, eternally.

A thousand words can't express,
The depth of love, I must confess,
That I feel for you, with all my heart,
Our love, a bond, that will never part.

In your eyes, I see my soul,
My heart beats for you, it's out of control,
With every breath, with every thought,
You're the one for whom I have fought.

Your touch, your smile, your gentle ways,
Fill my heart with endless praise,
You complete me, in every way,
In your love, I'll forever stay.

A thousand words may not suffice,
To express my love, so pure and nice,
But know this, my love, it's true,
I'll always love, forever you.

Your Love
Your love is like the sun that shines,
Brightening my days and warming my heart.
It's like a gentle breeze that caresses my skin,
A soothing touch that makes my troubles depart.
Your love is like the moon that glows,
Guiding me through the darkness of night.
It's like a symphony that sings to my soul,
A sweet melody that fills me with delight.

Your love is like a rose in bloom,
Fragrant and lovely, a sight to behold.
It's like a rainbow after the rain,
A promise of hope, a story untold.

Your love is everything to me,
A treasure that I cherish with all my heart.
I am grateful for every moment we share,
And for the love that we'll never part.

My Love, My Heart
My love for you is like a flame,
Burning bright, never to be tamed.
It warms my heart, it fills my soul,
It makes me feel complete and whole.
My heart beats for you, my love,
With every breath, I'm closer to heaven above.
I dream of you, day and night,
And in your arms, everything feels right.

My love for you is like a rose,
Soft petals, sweet fragrance, delicate and close.
I will nurture it, keep it alive,
For you are the one I want by my side.

My heart belongs to you, my love,
It beats for you, like wings of a dove.
I will love you always, until the end of time,
For you are my love, my heart, my rhyme.

You are My World
You are the sunshine on my face,
The sweet embrace that warms my heart.
You are the air that I breathe,
The reason why I never want to depart.
You are the beat in my heart,
The rhythm that guides me through the dark.
You are the star that lights up my night,
The beauty that keeps me in flight.

You are my world, my everything,
The one who makes my heart sing.
I am grateful for every moment we share,
And for the love that we both declare.

You are my love, my heart, my soul,
The one who makes me feel whole.
I will cherish you, always and forever,
For you are the reason why I never say never.

My heart beats for you
With every breath I take
You are my soulmate, my love
My life is complete with you by my side

Your eyes sparkle like stars
Your smile brightens up my day
I am so grateful to have you
In my life to stay

You are the sun to my day
The moon to my night
You complete me in every way
And make everything feel just right

Your touch sends shivers down my spine
Your kiss leaves me breathless and divine
You are my one and only love
My heart beats for you, my dove

You are the one I want to spend
The rest of my life with
Together we will weather any storm
And our love will always be a warm, bright
light.

Your Love
Your love is a beacon in the night,
Guiding me towards its warm light.
It fills my heart with hope and joy,
And makes my life feel complete and
buoy.

My Heart
My heart beats for you and you alone,
My love for you will never be overthrown.
I'll hold you close and keep you near,
And cherish you each day, my dear.

Sweet Embrace
In your sweet embrace I find,
A peace that calms my troubled mind.
Your love is like a gentle breeze,
Whispering softly through the trees.

Endless Love
My love for you will never die,
It soars high and reaches the sky.
It's like a flame that never fades,
Burning bright, with passion unafraid.

Forever
Forever, my love, I'll be true,
Forever, I'll love only you.
In this world of constant change,
Our love will remain, forever the same.

In the depths of my heart,
A flame burns bright and true,
For you, my sweet love,
My heart beats only for you.

Your smile lights up my world,
Your touch sets my soul ablaze,
With you by my side,
I am lost in a sweet daze.

Oh, my love, how I cherish you,
My heart is yours forevermore,
I vow to love you always,
Till the end of time and more.

My love, my heart beats for you,
Like the rhythm of a gentle song,
With each breath I take,
My love for you grows strong.

Your eyes, they sparkle like the stars,
Your touch, it sets my soul on fire,
Oh, my love, how you complete me,
My heart, it's filled with desire.

I long to hold you in my arms,
To feel your heart beating next to mine,
For in your embrace,
I find a love that's divine.

My love, you are the light of my life,
The one who makes everything right,
I vow to love you forever,
Till the end of time and beyond.

In your eyes, I see my future,
A love that's pure and true,
For you, my heart beats faster,
With each passing day anew.

Your touch, it sets my heart aflame,
Your smile, it melts my soul,
Oh, my love, how I adore you,
You make my world whole.

I'll love you through the ups and downs,
Through the laughter and the tears,
For you are the one I cherish,
The one who calms my fears.

My love, I'll be by your side always,
Through thick and thin, come what may,
For in your arms, I find my home,
My love for you will never stray.

In you I find a gentle grace
A beauty that shines from within
With each passing day, my love grows
As you fill my life with joy and hope.

Your smile, your laugh, your touch
All bring a warmth to my heart
A light that brightens even the darkest day
And makes everything feel right.

You are my heart, my soul, my everything
The one who makes my life complete
And I promise to love you always
Until the end of time and beyond.

When I first saw you, my heart skipped a beat
And I knew I had found something sweet
In your eyes, I saw a world of wonder
A love that would never go asunder.

Your gentle touch, your loving embrace
Has filled my life with beauty and grace
Each moment with you is a precious gift
A love that is pure and true, with no rift.

Together we will journey through life
Through its ups and downs, its joys and strife
For in your arms I find my peace
And a love that will never cease.

Your love is like a warm summer breeze
That fills my heart with joy and ease
With you, my life is complete
A love that is pure, honest and sweet.

In your eyes, I see a reflection
Of the love that we share, with no objection
With each passing day, my love for you grows
And with you, I know I've found my rose.

Together we will walk hand in hand
Through the valleys, the mountains, the sand
For in your arms, I find my home
A love that will always roam.

Your eyes are stars that light up my night,
Your smile a sun that warms my heart,
With you by my side, everything's right,
And I never want us to be apart.

You are the rose that blooms in my
garden,
The melody that plays in my heart,
With you, my life is full of magic,
And I never want us to be apart.

Your touch ignites a fire within me,
Your kiss a sweet symphony,
With you, I feel like I can conquer the
world,
And I never want us to be apart.

You are the moon that shines on my path,
The wind that carries me to new heights,
With you, my heart beats with joy,
And I never want us to be apart.

In the depths of my love, you'll find
A warmth that melts the coldest mind
A flame that burns both bright and true
A passion that's meant only for you

With each beat of my heart, I sigh
For the love that I feel inside
It's a feeling that words can't describe
A love that will never subside

I'll hold you close, so you can feel
The love that I have for you, so real
And every moment that we share
Will be a memory that we'll always wear

The beauty of your soul shines bright
Like a beacon in the darkest night
It draws me in, it captivates
And leaves me in a dreamlike state

Your eyes, they sparkle like the stars
And when you smile, it erases scars
The sound of your laughter is music to my ears
And it's a melody that I want to hear for years

You bring joy to my life every day
And with you, I know that I'm okay
So, let me love you with all that I am
For you're the only one who truly understands

With each passing day, I love you more
And my heart is yours forevermore
I'll cherish every moment that we share
And show you just how much I care

I'll be your rock, your shelter from the storm
And hold you close when the world is warm
I'll be your partner in this life
And love you more than words can describe

So take my hand and hold it tight
And know that I'll be there, day or night
For you're the love of my life, my heart
And I promise to love you, from the start.

In your eyes, I see the stars
The way you smile, it feels like ours
With every touch, I feel your heart
In your embrace, I find my art

The way you love, it fills my soul
Your touch, it makes me whole
Your heart, it beats with mine
With you, I feel just fine

Your love, it flows like a river
It's pure and true, it makes me shiver
With every kiss, I feel the heat
Your touch, it makes my heart skip a beat

Your eyes, they light up my world
Your touch, it makes my heart swirl
With every breath, I feel alive
With you, I know I'll survive

In your arms, I find my peace
With your love, my fears release
The way you touch, it's pure bliss
Your love, it's something I can't miss

With every word, you steal my heart
With every kiss, we never part
Your love, it's like a symphony
In your embrace, I find my harmony

Your love, it's like a fairytale
It's something I can't help but inhale
With every moment, I fall more
With every touch, my heart soars

Your smile, it's like the sun
Your love, it's never done
With every breath, I feel your soul
With you, I know I'm whole

The beauty of your love
Is like the morning sun
Radiant and warm
Filling my life with light
You are the one I cherish
The one I hold dear
My love for you will never fade
It will only grow stronger with each passing year

Your love is a song
That echoes in my heart
A melody that lingers
Even when we're apart
I close my eyes and listen
To the sweet sound of your voice
And I know that I am lucky
To have you as my choice.

Your love is my life
The reason I wake up each day
It gives me hope and strength
And shows me the way
Without you, I am lost
A ship without a sail
But with you, I am whole
And my heart will never fail

Love is a beautiful thing
A feeling that fills the soul
It makes us feel alive
And helps us reach our goal
With you, I feel complete
Like I've found my missing part
Together we can conquer anything
And hold each other's heart

My love for you is like a flame
That burns bright and true
It warms my heart and fills my soul
And guides me back to you
With every breath I take
And every beat of my heart
I promise to love you
Till the end of time, till we're never apart.

As endless as the ocean's blue,
My love for you will always be true,
Across the mountains and through the skies,
My love for you will never die.

Through every storm and every breeze,
My love for you will never cease,
Across the years and through the days,
My love for you will always stay.

So take my hand and come with me,
Together we'll journey endlessly,
Through every moment, every place,
My love for you will light our way.

My heart beats for you, my love,
In every moment, every day,
You are the sunshine in my life,
The reason why my heart can sway.

Your smile is like the morning sun,
That brightens up my darkest day,
Your laughter is the sweetest sound,
That takes all my worries away.

I'll cherish you forevermore,
My love for you will never fade,
Together we'll face every challenge,
And make each other's hearts elated.

With every breath, with every beat,
My love for you will always meet,
Your eyes are like the stars above,
That sparkle with undying love.

Your touch ignites a fire in me,
That burns with passion endlessly,
With every moment that we share,
My love for you will always be there.

So take my heart and keep it close,
Forever yours, I make this toast,
In every moment, every way,
My love for you will never stray.

My love for you will never fade,
It's as constant as the stars above.
It burns brighter every day,
And fills my heart with so much love.

With every beat of my heart,
I feel your love deep inside.
I never want us to be apart,
And with you, my heart will abide.

Together we'll weather any storm,
Our love will stand the test of time.
I'm grateful you were born,
And I'm yours, forever and always, mine.

Your love is like a summer breeze,
Soft and gentle, it puts me at ease.
With you, I feel alive and free,
And every moment spent with you is ecstasy.

I am forever grateful,
That you came into my life.
You make everything beautiful,
And fill my days with light.

With you, I know I am safe,
And everything will be okay.
Your love is my refuge,
And with you, I want to stay.

We are soulmates, you and I,
Destined to be together until we die.
Our love is pure and true,
And nothing can ever change it, no matter what we do.

With you, I am complete,
And together we can conquer defeat.
You are the missing piece of my heart,
And with you, I can never fall apart.

Our love is like a beacon of light,
Guiding us through the darkest night.
I am forever yours, and you are mine,
Together we will forever shine.

My heart belongs to you, my love,
With every beat it sings your name,
My thoughts are filled with thoughts of you,
And nothing else can bring me the same.

Your touch ignites a flame in me,
That burns with passion bright and true,
And in your arms I find the peace,
That only comes from being with you.

So take my hand and walk with me,
Through life's uncertain twists and turns,
For as long as we're together,
Our love will always brightly burn.

In your eyes I see a love,
That fills my heart with joy and light,
A love that lifts me up so high,
And makes everything feel right.

Your smile, it lights up my world,
And your touch, it sends shivers down my spine,
With you beside me, I feel complete,
And nothing else can compare to thine.

I'll cherish every moment spent with you,
And hold onto your love so true,
For you are the only one I need,
And I'll always be devoted to you.

Our love is like a symphony,
Each note and chord in perfect harmony,
It fills my soul with such sweet sound,
And lifts my heart off the ground.

With every kiss and every touch,
Our passion soars, it's never too much,
For in your arms, I feel so free,
And I know that you were made for me.

So let us dance to love's sweet tune,
And let our hearts beat as one soon,
For in your love I've found my home,
And with you, I'll never be alone.

The beauty of your love,
Is like a rose in bloom,
With every petal opening,
My heart is consumed.

The fire of your love,
Burns bright within my heart,
With every touch and kiss,
Our passion never departs.

In your arms, I find my home,
Where I'm safe and loved and never alone,
With you by my side, my heart's at ease,
For in your love, I've found my peace.

My love is like a song,
That echoes in your heart,
With every note and every chord,
Our love will never depart.

The depths of your love,
Are like the ocean blue,
Endless and unyielding,
My heart belongs to you.

A love so true, it shines so bright,
It fills my heart with such delight,
With every beat, my love for you,
Grows stronger, pure and ever true.

The sweetness of your love,
Is like a candy treat,
With every taste and every bite,
My love for you, it can't be beat.

The light of your love,
Illuminates my life,
With every touch and every kiss,
My heart takes flight.

Our love is like a symphony,
Each note and chord in perfect harmony,
It fills my soul with such sweet sound,
And lifts my heart off the ground.

My heart beats for you,
With every breath I take,
For in your love, I've found my soulmate,
And my heart will never break.

In your eyes, I see a love,
That fills my heart with joy and light,
A love that lifts me up so high,
And makes everything feel right.

My forever love, you are my heart,
My soulmate, my better part,
With you by my side, I am complete,
And our love will never miss a beat.

The magic of your love,
Is like a fairytale dream,
With every moment spent with you,
My heart bursts at the seams.

Your love is my anchor,
That keeps me steady and strong,
With you by my side, I know I can face,
Anything that life brings along.

The grace of your love,
Is like a butterfly's wings,
So delicate and beautiful,
My heart takes flight and sings.

In your eyes, I see the sun,
And in your arms, I feel the warmth;
My love for you is infinite,
A flame that will never die.

With every beat of my heart,
I pledge my love to you;
Forever and always, my darling,
My heart beats for you.

In your embrace, I find my home,
A place of safety and warmth;
Your love is a light that guides me,
Through the darkest of storms.

With every kiss, my heart soars,
Higher than the highest star;
Your touch ignites a flame within me,
A flame that burns for all time.

In your arms, I am complete,
Whole and happy and free;
My love for you is boundless,
And always will be.

Love is a magic that fills the soul,
A feeling that words cannot express;
It transforms the ordinary into the extraordinary,
And makes every moment a treasure.

In your smile, I see the beauty of life,
And in your touch, I feel the power of love;
Your love is a gift that I cherish,
A precious gem beyond measure.

Together, we are stronger than the stars,
And our love is a force that can move mountains;
In each other's arms, we find the strength,
To face the world and all its challenges.

In your arms, I find my home,
A place where I'm not alone.
Your embrace is warm and tight,
And I know everything will be alright.

With every kiss, my heart takes flight,
And I feel like I'm walking on clouds at night.
Your love is like a precious gem,
A treasure that I'll cherish until the end.

My heart beats for you, my love,
As steady as the sun above.
No matter where life takes me,
You're the one I want to be with, you see.

With every moment that we share,
I feel like I'm walking on air.
Your love is like a river deep,
A feeling that I can't help but keep.

You are my everything, my heart and soul,
The one who makes me feel whole.
With you by my side, I can conquer anything,
And face the challenges that life may bring.

Your smile brightens up my darkest days,
And your touch sets my heart ablaze.
I thank the stars above for bringing you to me,
And I vow to love you for eternity.

The beauty of your love is like a rose,
Delicate and fragrant, yet strong and bold.
It fills my heart with joy and bliss,
And I can't help but be grateful for this.

With every moment that we share,
I feel like I'm walking on air.
Your love is like a gentle breeze,
A feeling that puts my mind at ease.

Together forever, you and I,
A love that will never die.
Through thick and thin, we'll stand by each other,
And face every challenge, together.

Your love is like a beacon of light,
Guiding me through the darkest night.
With you by my side, I know I can do anything,
And I'll love you until the end of time.

In your embrace, I find solace and peace
My heart races, my pulse starts to increase
You're the missing piece, the puzzle complete
In your eyes, my reflection I meet

With every breath, my love for you grows
My heart overflows, my passion shows
You're the fire that sets my soul ablaze
The love we share, an eternal maze

I see you and my heart skips a beat
Your smile, your touch, so sweet and neat
My love for you, a never-ending stream
The stuff of fairytales and dreams

With every word, every glance, every touch
My love for you, I cannot hide or clutch
You are the sun that brightens my day
My love for you, it will never fade away

Your beauty, a masterpiece, a work of art
Your soul, a treasure, a piece of my heart
My love for you, an endless ocean blue
Together forever, just me and you

With every breath, every step, every move
My love for you, it will never subdue
You're the star that shines bright in my sky
My love for you, it will never die.

My love for you is like a flame
That burns both bright and true
It flickers and it dances
And it's always there for you

I'll keep it burning steadily
And let it guide the way
For every step we take together
And every single day

So know that you can count on me
To be your guiding light
And keep our love alight and strong
Through every day and night

Your smile is like the sunshine
That brightens up my day
It warms my heart and fills my soul
And takes my breath away

Your touch is like a gentle breeze
That sweeps across my skin
It sends a shiver down my spine
And makes my heart begin

To beat a little faster
With every passing moment
For in your arms I feel at home
And never feel so broken

So let me hold you close to me
And never let you go
For with you here beside me
I feel like I'm home

My love for you is like the stars
That shine so bright and clear
It twinkles in my heart and soul
And makes my love so dear

I'll wrap my arms around you
And hold you close and tight
And never let you go my dear
Through every day and night

For you are like the moon and stars
That light up all my skies
And make me feel so loved and cherished
With every beat of my heart's cries

So let me be your shining star
That guides you through the night
And be the one who loves you most
With every ounce of my might.

Of all the emotions that we feel,
Love is the one that makes us reel.
It brings us joy and makes us whole,
Filling our hearts and lighting our soul.

With you by my side, I feel complete,
Your love is the one thing I'll always keep.
Your touch, your kiss, your warm embrace,
They all take me to a heavenly place.

Like a rose in bloom, your beauty shines,
Your smile, your eyes, they're all divine.
And when you speak, your voice is like music,
My heart beats faster, and I can't refuse it.

With every passing day, my love for you grows,
Like a river that flows, it never slows.
I'll cherish you always, and hold you near,
For your love is what I hold most dear.

In the depths of my heart, there's a flame,
Burning bright, calling out your name.
It fills me with warmth, it fills me with love,
Guiding me to you, like the stars above.

With you by my side, the world is so bright,
Everything's better, everything's just right.
Your smile, your laugh, they light up my day,
And I'll do anything, just to make you stay.

Your love is a treasure, a precious gem,
And I'll protect it always, like a priceless emblem.
I'll be your rock, your shelter from the storm,
And I'll hold you close, until the night is gone.

For your love is the one thing I'll always need,
Like water to a flower, it's what makes me breathe.
So let us walk together, hand in hand,
For our love is forever, and nothing can withstand..

Love is like a rose, with petals soft and pure,
Its beauty is so fleeting, so delicate, so sure.
It blooms and fades, like the passing of time,
But its essence remains, like a sweet summer rhyme.

Your love is the sun, that warms my soul,
It brightens my day, and makes me whole.
Your smile, your touch, they fill me with light,
And in your arms, everything's all right.

Like a river that flows, your love is so strong,
It carries me through life, where I belong.
Your heart is my home, my sanctuary, my peace,
And I'll love you always, without any cease.

So let us cherish every moment, every day,
For life is so short, and time slips away.
Let us love each other, with all our might,
And we'll be together, until the end of the night.

My heart beats for you, my love,
With each pulse, I feel your touch.
I'm lost in your eyes, your smile, your kiss,
My heart belongs to you, I confess.

I never thought I'd find a love so true,
A love that fills me through and through.
But here I am, with you by my side,
And I know my heart will never hide.

For you are the one who makes my heart sing,
You are the one who gives me wings.
I'll love you forever, my sweetest one,
Until the end of time, till the day is done.

The beauty of your love is like a rose,
So sweet and fragrant, it overflows.
Your love is like the sun, so warm and bright,
It fills my heart with such delight.

Your touch is like a gentle breeze,
It soothes my soul and puts me at ease.
Your smile is like a ray of light,
It brightens up my darkest night.

My love for you is like a song,
A melody that's never wrong.
I'll sing it loud, I'll sing it proud,
My love for you will never be allowed.

For you are the one who makes my heart beat,
You are the one who makes my life complete.
I'll cherish you forever, my precious dove,
For the beauty of your love.

Your love is my everything,
My reason for living, my reason for being.
With you by my side, I'm never alone,
Your love is my home, my heart's only throne.

Your touch is like a gentle caress,
It fills me with such tenderness.
Your kiss is like a flame that ignites,
It sets my heart and soul alight.

I'll never let you go, my dearest one,
I'll hold you close, till the day is done.
For you are my everything, my heart and soul,
My love for you will never grow old.

So let me love you, let me cherish you,
Let me hold you close, till the end of time is due.
For your love is my everything, my sweetest dream,
And I'll love you forever, my love supreme.

In your eyes, I see the stars,
In your touch, I feel the sun,
In your embrace, I find solace,
With you, my love, I am undone.

Your smile is the sun that warms my day,
Your laughter, the music that fills my soul,
Your love, the light that guides my way,
With you, my heart is whole.

When I am with you, my heart sings,
With every beat, it calls your name,
Your love is the joy that my heart brings,
With you, my love, I'll never be the same.

In your arms, I find my rest,
With your love, I am blessed,
Every moment spent with you,
Is a moment cherished, pure and true.

In your eyes, I see my future,
With your heart, I find my home,
Your love is the anchor that keeps me
steady,
With you, my love, I'll never roam.

My heart beats a melody,
A song of love so sweet,
With each note, my love for you
Becomes more complete.

In every whispered word I speak,
In every tender touch,
I tell you how much I love you,
With the language of love.

In your arms, I find my home,
A place of love and grace,
With every embrace, I'm reminded
Of the beauty of your face.

My heart beats for you, my love,
With every breath I take.
I never thought I'd find someone
As wonderful as you to make
My days brighter and my nights warmer,
My life full of love and laughter.
You're the missing piece of my puzzle,
The one I've been searching for after.

You are the sunshine of my life,
The one who makes my heart sing.
You're the reason I wake up every morning,
And the one who makes my heart take wing.
Your smile brightens up my darkest days,
Your touch sets my soul on fire.
With you by my side, I feel invincible,
And my love for you will never expire.

In your eyes, I see a world of wonder,
A place where love and beauty reign.
I feel your touch and I am transported
To a realm where joy knows no pain.
You are the moon and the stars to me,
The one who makes my life complete.
I love you more with each passing moment,
And I will never let you go or retreat.

I never knew what love was
Until I met you, my sweet.
You are the one who makes my heart beat,
And my soul skip a beat.
Your beauty takes my breath away,
And your love makes me complete.
I thank the universe every day
For bringing you into my life, my sweet.

"Infinite Love"

In your eyes, I see the stars
In your touch, I feel the sun
In your smile, I find my joy
In your love, I've just begun

You are my heart, my soul, my all
My partner, my lover, my friend
Our love is like the universe
It has no beginning, it has no end

I promise to cherish you forever
And love you more with each passing day
For in your arms, I've found my home
And in your love, I'll always stay

"Soulmates"

You are the one my heart beats for
The one my soul longs to adore
My partner, my friend, my confidant
In your love, I find my haven

We are two souls intertwined
Destined to be together, divine
Our love is a symphony, a masterpiece
Written in the stars for all to see

With each passing moment, I'm grateful
For your love, your kindness, your grace
I thank the universe for bringing us together
And making us soulmates, forever and always